The Infinite Park

OTHER BOOKS BY PETER UNWIN

The Rock Farmers (SHORT STORIES, 1994)

Nine Bells For A Man (NOVEL, 2000)

The Wolf's Head: Writing Lake Superior (2008)

Hard Surface: In Search of the Canadian Road (2009)

Life Without Death (SHORT STORIES, 2013)

Canadian Folk: Portraits of Remarkable Lives (2013)

Written in Stone (2020)

The Infinite Park

poems by Peter Unwin

Cormorant Books

This is a first edition.

We acknowledge financial support for our publishing activities: the Government of Canada through the Canada Book Fund and The Canada Council for the Arts; the Government of Ontario, through the Ontario Arts Council, Ontario Creates, and the Ontario Book Publishing Tax Credit. We acknowledge additional funding provided by the Government of Ontario and the Ontario Arts Council to address the adverse effects of the novel coronavirus pandemic.

LIBRARY AND ARCHIVES CANADA CATALOGUING IN PUBLICATION

Title: The infinite park / poems by Peter Unwin.
Names: Unwin, Peter, 1956– author.
Identifiers: Canadiana 20200340328 | ISBN 9781770866065 (softcover)
Classification: LCC PS8591.N94 I54 2021 | DDC C811/.54—dc23

Cover art and design: Angel Guerra / Archetype
Interior text design: Tannice Goddard, tannicegdesigns.ca
Printer: Sunville Printco

Printed and bound in Canada.

The interior of this book is printed on 100% post-consumer waste recycled paper.

CORMORANT BOOKS INC.
260 SPADINA AVENUE, SUITE 502, TORONTO, ONTARIO, M5T 2E4
www.cormorantbooks.com

It is my privilege to thank the people in these poems for what they have granted to life and to me. For their love and the passion and the laughter and sometimes for the indifference, and for everything that we have inflicted on each other. My daughters and my wife who make up the skin and bones of this poetry and who taught me how to wash my hands. Friendships that exist on either side of language and some of which exist no more. The animals that came to my door wearing the face of hunger. There are hardly enough words to acknowledge the debts that I have incurred in a single day and in a single poem. I wish to thank everyone of you for what you have given to me.

PETER UNWIN, TORONTO, 2021

CONTENTS

The Infinite Park

HOUSE POEMS

HE COULD HAVE BEEN ANYONE

I still wash and dry the shirts
of a man named Philip dead
twenty years; he was given
to grand mal seizures
mini putt golf and the most
difficult acrostics he could
get his hands on.

He had cruised timber
up the Montreal River
and crashed one light aircraft
after another before retiring
into real estate.

He approached life
as an opportunity to worry.
He had been abused as a child
but there was an understandable
reluctance to see how that fit
with his current life.

Life entailed obligations
to be a man. He did his best
in that regard but the rules
were vague; they came to him
muffled from behind bedroom doors.

The house remained clean
but there was no love in it.
There was love but it was love

avant la lettre so to speak.
The way animals died on a trap line
up the Goulais River is the way
love expressed itself in that home.

The other homes were dark too.
No one was equipped to handle
the world. The world
had everybody by the throat.
The women were not safe in it.
The men didn't have a clue.
Only the children remained passionate
in their dark rooms.

LOST

Once again everything is lost;
the wallet, the keys, the sapphire ring
that fell between the floorboards
of the gymnasium, youth, good looks,
casual sex, the continent of Atlantis ...
All of it has fallen behind the cushions
of the sofa that used to be in the living room.

My father lost four fingers off his left hand.
My mother tragically lost her mind, my daughter
lost her iPod Nano the day we bought it for her.
My next door neighbour lost her husband, never did
find him, except for alternate weekends.

I lost my innocence when I was sixteen
to a girl who lost hers when she was fourteen.
I have lost touch with her. The truth is
I lost her to another man. Last night in the dark
I lost my confidence and not for the first time either.

WHEN YOU WERE SIX

I meant to write of you once
When you were six how the city
Made you strong and the streets
Nourished you, I meant to write
Of your mother and father
How they could only gasp
at what you were.

But I did not write of you I wrote
Of roads and rivers and a man
Who could no longer tolerate
The beauty of a woman and so
Lived in a machine. And when
Finally I came to write of you
The book was dead or at least
It was not feeling very well
And you were singing
At the top of your lungs.

LIVING IN A RUINED HOUSE

Once again our house is in ruins
Only this time neither of us is young.
The heavens explode over our heads
The roof somehow does not leak even though
The roofer died of a heart attack
Halfway through the job.

Next door a husband abdicates his house
And his children. His attractive wife
Is heartbroken. Their house is ruined;
Every second weekend the man returns
And for fifteen minutes there is an
Uncomfortable rapprochement on the lawn.

I long ago lost the energy to leave you;
I'm not sure you would notice if I did.
We live in this ruined house together.
You have lost your job, I never had one
To begin with. How will we feed ourselves
Or fix our ruined house? Goddess will look
After us you used to say, but Goddess
Has had a sex change and the house
Of heaven is in ruins too. What will we do?

What will we do? Who will pay for the children's
Data plans? Soon I will be dead, you too. Who
Can afford that? Neither of us factored in being dead.
Yesterday I found an arrowhead
In the back yard; probably it was once buried
In the brain of a mastodon.

WINDY DAYS

They called for winds
Of one hundred and forty kilometres an hour
Wind enough to remove your eyes
From your head.

It rattled the roof alright
And made the tree branches beckon
Like witchy broomsticks.
We've ruined the world I'm afraid

All we have to show for it
Are a few gaudy houses
On the Bridle Path
That no one can afford.

The wind blew my bedroom slippers
Out the window and hell
Broke loose. A lone voice sang
"fly me to the moon"

And I recognized the voice,
My daughter must have been in the house
Somewhere. We blew down the street
Like tumbleweed singing

Fly me to the moon
Or anything else that came to mind.
So much for everything being in order
Life had become a catastrophe

Of half-baked opinions clung to
With both fists. Everyone was indignant
And letting everyone know.

Nonetheless your hair in the wind
Was a monument to being alive
Wild in the wind that blew
Your hair around your face
Like the face of a young woman.

We were born to play
In wind like this. Great frozen wind
That bangs the house and brings the room
Down around our knees.

REFUGEES

Who would have thought you'd
find your refuge matching unmatched
socks on a Sunday afternoon, having
just returned from the funeral of a woman
you met only three times and who had,
herself, buried three husbands.
Stark raving mad at the end, her mind
had turned to sauce but she was not
violent, for which the staff was grateful.
"Dignity is what we're after in these
dark times" spoke her son at the funeral. Dignity
and maybe a whiff of something else.

MIRACLES

To be well fed on fish and new potatoes
is a miracle, to go upstairs
with a ceramic pot in one hand
and D'Aulaire's *Book of Greek Myths*
in the other is a miracle. The faint
smell of urine is miraculous
as is grouting between old timbers
and spiders levitating across water.
Miraculous are the dead; mother, other
women; Bruce, the little boy
struck by a car was a miracle
as is the sinewy trace of a wood match
scribbled on stove blacking
and the urge to say, or paint
or be immersed in water, to name
stars, slam doors, don strange
hats and to instantly like someone
introduced in a restaurant.

THE BASTARD

I sensed something strong
Had entered the morning. The woman
Lay on the sofa marking papers.
I had embarrassed myself
The night before and she
Greeted me evenly.
I thought again how lucky
I was to be with her and how
I'd pushed that luck to the limit.

I had come into the morning
Intent on forgiving myself
But that was not possible
No matter how I tried
I had no choice but to despise
That bastard for what he'd done
to her and to me too.

HOW ARE YOU FEELING

"My god your hair is beautiful,"
he said, "the way it crests like that.
Would you consider marrying me
or having my children, I mean *your* children
or giving me your number? Please," he said,
"you are so beautiful it's a wonder I haven't written
several books about you."

"We met ten minutes ago," she said skeptically
but the time of the skeptics was over.
Love was back in the air and in the smell
of her laundry about which he possessed
an alarming interest.

"What then," he cried. "Are we just
to grow old and die like every other
sucker on this planet?" "Yes," she said,
"yes, we are."

"Well, let's get at it then," he said,
"though I should warn you I'm not
feeling very well." "That's alright,"
she said, "I'm not feeling that great
either."

THE BLUE TRAIN

Coltrane's Blue Train is in my ear
A full moon is in the sky
Who am I to choose?

Who am I to even get out of bed
When the wind fondles the forest

And the girl in the next room
Can be heard fingering
The pages
Of yet another book?

Living in the country has never been so free
No shotgun blasts, no broken marriages
Coltrane has never swung that thing

With such alacrity. At what point
Did I ask for bread instead of stones
And by whose grace did I get it?

GIRL SINGING TO HORSES

When she could sing but not yet talk
She stood at the wire fence singing
To the horses. Indifferent at first
One or two of them cast dubious
Neck-long glances her way
And stared without interest.

She sang the song every child knows;
The one that never ends and because the song
Never ended the horses one after another
Took notice, they put their heavy eyes
On her until all of them stood transfixed

By the two-legged child filling the air
With horse music. They paused at their cropping
And turned to face her, a small face
Filling up the field

With what they'd heard before
And forgotten but now remembered;
That song that never ended
And reminded them
Who they were.

THE FRIENDS WE MADE

Any one of them might be reached by phone
their faces can appear out of the air
without prompting. Every thing
that you did no matter how many years ago
retains the ability to take the swagger
out of your brisk morning walk to the subway.
Did you think people would say, "Oh him,
he was the one who walked briskly to the subway."
Did you think you fooled anyone?
You barely fooled yourself.

In the end there's nothing like the friendship of friends
no matter how much you pride yourself
on your ability to withstand outrageous
and usually self-inflicted misfortune.
There is nothing that matches
the delightfulness of that woman's laugh
when she committed it in your presence
and you had no reason to believe
your friendship wouldn't last forever.

THE PAINTERLY LIFE

What happened to that portrait of me
That you painted when you were still alive
Before the accident, prior to the phone call,
When things were right-side up although
Beginning to tilt perceptibly in the other direction?

Those days when we skated on the canal
And the kittens ran wild in our rented rooms.
Did time run out on those times? Can no more
Juice be squeezed from those lemons?

What happened to that painting of me
That parody of a Roman emperor, bare-chested
With a crown of laurel leaves painted on my head?
Where is it now? In what city? Where are you?
Where's that plastic leaf-shaped crown
You painted on my head when you made me king?

WAX FOR 24 POINTS

He weathered the storm in a tent
with his daughter playing Scrabble
until he couldn't take it anymore.

"Wax for twenty-four points," she said
and he knew he would lose. He always
lost to her.

He wanted the rain to make him
a better person. Nothing happened
that way but the tarp held

and they both awoke
in the morning without a drop
on them.

GREAT BALLS OF FIRE

We were the speed kills generation.
The gloves had come off.
So had the pants.
You could say it was free love
all the way to the bank.

I'm not saying it was all good.
There were venomous arguments
that spilled across lawns.
There were scenes in pawn shops
worthy of Rod Steiger.

Mom sobbed a lot.
Dad had issues with anger management
which is not what we called it back then.
We called it get out of the house fast.

FURTHERMORE

Even though the war had ended fifteen years ago
the town still stank of it.

The town had a history of course.
Any town that says it doesn't is lying to you.
A dog was set on fire in that town
during the Rebellion of 1837
when the rebels hid in the caves
of the limestone cliffs. Mighty Niagara
roared as loudly as a kid's drunk dad
and kisses were to be had at the roller rink.

Fights broke out over girls
or with them, and it's a wonder nobody
we knew got pregnant and if they did
there was a home ten miles out of town
where they went until the thing blew over.

The saints were called upon frequently
and sometimes a terrifying phone call
pierced the house when everyone was sleeping.
The old mills crumbled and went away
leaving the factories empty although the suckers
still ran in the creeks and smelt were netted
in a strange ritual of men in waders
beating the water with sticks.

Sometimes a house
went dark and stayed that way although we knew
someone was in there saving on electricity
or sobbing. When the lights went out
and the baked goods stopped emerging from the oven
we knew the woman who lived there was a witch.

GENERATIONAL

Children are not so great
But they're not the end of the world either.
The truth is that children are always
on their way to being something else.
They're neither here nor there.
Up to a certain age it's clear
They're going straight to heaven.
After that it would be nice if they left
The house for a few days.

We know that children are wise
Because they sleep a great deal. We know
They're human because they resemble us
In ways they would rather not. Children
Are necessary because they make the old man
bend his creaky knees and rise from his chair;
"Play a game with us," the children cry. "We will
Hide in the future and you can spend
the rest of your life looking for us."

EXACTLY LIKE THIS

When I'm dead and gone I suspect
It will be exactly like this; the constant
Surf of traffic beneath the balcony
The bang of a child's fingers on the piano,
Another child vexing her bow
Against the violin, the mind brimming
With ideas. Only a half-filled glass
Of beer will be absent from this picture
The dead do not drink beer to my knowledge
Perhaps they smoke a little weed, exchange
Dubious photographs of each other's spouses
But for the most part they don't get drunk
The way they did when they weren't dead.
For the most part they behave themselves
Like the parents in the books I read
To my kids.

HOW I MET MY WIFE

When being young was a full time job
I found myself gainfully employed
As a shoe salesman. This allowed me to glance
Up the skirts of many women
And preserve the illusions of both youth
And lingerie but it did not prepare me
In any meaningful way for my life.

For that it was necessary to quit my job
And line up in front of a counter where state
Subsidized medications were issued
To the elderly. Here the elegant
Heels of troubling young beauties
Played no part beyond their tap-tappings
In memory, and we kept
Our eyeballs buried in our smart phones
While waiting for our numbers to be called.

But it turns out there aren't enough numbers
For the old and we were issued names
Which none of us remember anymore.
What I remember is the snap of leather
Fitting over her perfect heel and her
Cool appraisal in the mirror
As she gauged precisely where she stood.

THE PROS AND CONS OF MY HUSBAND

When I met him the world was a less
Thirsty place. He was a drenched
Fair-haired man and change was afoot.
He courted me with books and said
I possessed a beauty that surpassed
His foolishness. We lived together
In broken cars and scratched records.
We swam Lake Superior and fought
Each other by the minute.

Soon I saw that no king was hidden
In this man. Whatever
Whale swallowed him had coughed
Him up quick enough to sleep in my bed
That's for sure.

He did however journey with me
To the woods and forest where the children
Were found. How frightened he was
To bring them home. But they're not ours
He said, they're not ours. Nothing
Is ours, I said, not even us.

WITHOUT YOU

I'm afraid that without you the cat
will get out of the bag. The horse
will escape the barn and the bats will exit
hell in a hurry. Without you I'm afraid
that a journey of a million miles will be reduced

to something we do one step at a time
and that no amount of rainwater
will make the garden grow again.
Please promise not to take up residence
in that neighbourhood no one comes back from.

The rents are out of whack there and children
are not allowed to holler in the hallways.
Please attend to me where I live in this
run-down house. At least here there is still room
to hide the dirt beneath the carpets.

THE DRUNKEN BED

The bed contained altogether
too much disappointment, too many
broken men had initiated too many
half measures that availed them not.
It sagged in the middle where the heavy
lifting got done. All that heaving
of the javelin etc., the cries of love,
some uttered in French, the poisonous
arguments the cats the dogs that climbed
on it in search of a face to lick, the kids
who came to it clutching their stuffies
and wanting in.

The bed tables stood guard on each side;
hers piled with Achebe, an illustrated
guide to Malta and its temples, three
novels all of them described as "unforgettable"
on the cover and a rattling great bottle
of painkillers. On his the collected letters
of an alcoholic writer dead for years
and an unopened jar of youth cream.

"This is our bed," she said, she was wedded
to its comfort. He knew only its great torment
and agonies. "There are mothballs in the bed,"
he cried but it was only the smell
of shampoo on the pillow. "Come to bed,"
she said. "Don't torment yourself
unnecessarily."

CONSIDER THE BEDSIDE TABLE

As if the bed isn't bad enough
consider the bedside table
the indiscretions it has witnessed;
the evidence that lies on top of it
the diaries that tell all, the lovers
who placed their contraceptives there
waiting for the right moment.

The bed is bad but the bedside table
is where it starts; the first place they dust
for fingerprints, the glass of water
that washes down God knows what
now contains countless bubbles of what
appears to be air.

Whose earrings are those anyways
and what are they doing on my bedside table?
Between the bed and the bedside table
A whole family can go missing.

GLADIATORS

After thirty years with you
I move less slowly
Toward the goals of my youth.
Ignorance is upon me;
Music terrorizes the night.
An idiotic game of shuffleboard
Is barely audible beneath the central air.
I have passed my prime
The way Pepys passed a kidney stone.
Home is where the kids are at, and the cats
I don't have to tell you that.
You know better than me
The responsibilities of growing old
The mind going soft, the going
Getting tough. The familiar mob
In the arena with its thumbs down
Brays for blood but secretly
They envy what we've done.

WHAT A RELIEF

The children are all grown up
Which is to say they are selfish, rude
And merciless toward any form of hypocrisy
But their own. The sonograms
Came back clean which is to say
I will not be looking to throw myself
Under a bus anytime soon. At least not this week.
Imagine a life without you, imagine
The world coming to an end
Not with a bang but with a cataclysmic
Kick in the head that leaves everyone
Deaf, dumb, and looking to hook up
With the first person who is remotely available.
The rain has stopped.
Old age, decrepitude and failing
Mental capacities have been banished
To the basement while the young ones
Are upstairs on the sofa making love
Like there's no tomorrow.

REAL ESTATES

They tore the house down
and put a hole there where Ray
and Linda used to live; odd ducks
both of them, him with his Scottish
dancing and her with her tightly tied
red hair.

They upped and skedaddled
I'm tempted to say to Schenectady
but of course it wasn't Schenectady
no one skedaddles to Schenectady anymore.
They moved to Hamilton instead. The rents
are cheap there. He had some work
with the university, the mathematics department
I believe or the Scottish dancing department.

On Halloween he came to my door
holding two drams and wearing a kilt.
She was Frieda Kahlo. She danced and sang.
We dished candy to the kids. We were not young.
I believe I once saw her secretly
stealing French fries from someone
else's plate at the steakhouse down the street
but I'm no longer sure.

There's so much not to be sure about.
Real estate has gone crazy.
The dilapidated shambles of a house
where they triaged the stray and injured
animals of the neighbourhood is demolished.
Just a pit now filled with rainwater. Men
slosh about in it wearing boots. They say
someone's going to make a fortune.

THINGS FALL APART

When things fell apart
We located ourselves in our crumpled bodies
And petted the cat with a new found intensity.
We were not animal lovers, not even lovers really
Just people who lay in bed together and inhaled
And exhaled, rose and fell, fought and made peace
Made breakfast, lunch and dinner and paid
Heavily for the mistakes of the past.

What remained was an 1878 edition
Of *The Book Lovers Enchiridion*
And a pressing urge to use the toilet.
Breakfast was on its way, you could count on that,
At least coffee. Certainly there were things
that needed doing, but what they were
Or who would do them was unclear.
The kids were asleep.
It wasn't a snow day but there they were.
Obviously some sort of happiness
Had found its way into the house
And had no intention of getting out of bed.

THE PARLIAMENT OF HOUSES

Morning alarms ring indicating the parliament
Of houses is about to reconvene.

The kids are groaning in their beds
The speaker of the house is downstairs

Assembling the coffee.
Rain bangs on the window. For the last

Several years the water pressure
Has made a high whining sound in the pipes.

No government is perfect. Our ministers
Are forever blackmailed because their hearts

Remain open to love and the alternative
Is something they refuse to live with.

WHO KNOWS

Who knows what waits for us
Once we arrive at that place?
Maybe an old fashioned steak
Cooked on the barbecue and a glass
Of lemonade left in the shade
By a considerate staff member.

Frozen rain has battered
The windows for several days. My daughter
Wants to know how much I love her.
Nine out of ten, I say and this seems
To satisfy her.

I make a point of saying I love you
Because you never know, and even
If you do it's nice to have the sound
Of a human voice knocking around
In the old house.

THE HARBOUR WOMAN

"Hey sailor," she said, "why don't
You and I go upscale?"
And with that she took out her bow
And started in on a little Rossini.

It wasn't the first time a woman
Had brought me face to face with music;
My daughters will not shut up
When it comes to singing and my wife

Had once been known for her set of pipes
Along with some other achievements
About which she is less than candid.
Still, the woman could play Rossini like a fiend

And life was coming to an end.
At least *mine* was. Everybody else
Seemed to be full speed ahead
Firing off one brilliant social media message

After another. No one even had time
To get cancer anymore let alone
Lie in bed sweating and paralyzed
By how their lives had come to nothing.

I listened, I watched her play
Her shoulders were bare of course;
The moon was doing something
And the stars were doing something too.

Then I was in the bedroom at dawn
It was raining outside and my wife
Stood rummaging in her top drawer
For something to put on.

LUCKY FELLOW

He certainly hauled a load of baggage
up and down those hills. He hauls it
still even though he's not out of bed yet.

The sun casts a thermonuclear hue
into the room. The door slams stormily
the way it does when a furious and indignant
teenager gets her hands on it.

He's reached the point where coffee is crucial.
Someone he loves isn't well, others he doesn't give
a damn about have ascended to high places.

He knows now that he lacked the wherewithal to achieve
culture. Maybe he memorized
a few lines of Wordsworth but what good
did it do when the truth spilled like beans
across the kitchen floor and he made
solemn promises that didn't last a day?

If not for the ability of women to get the job done
he'd still be sequestered in that dingy basement
with the mice, writing short fictions in the manner
of Pascal and living off a bag of Halloween candy.

RAIN

for S. Hughes

Nothing she could say or do
was not true and when she died
the men who loved her cried and vowed
to get their lives together
no matter what.

And no matter what we did
we didn't get our lives together
we didn't rise to the occasion.
Instead we dropped the ball or fell
flat on our faces, or stepped
out of bounds.

We allowed our memberships
to expire. We matriculated and had children
but in the end we knew the rain, when it came,
had come in response
to her absence.

MEMORY OF A MARITIME CAMP

The horse above the harbour
Never had been ridden they said
Or had been ridden but was now
Broken of the habit.

An old horse; the children
Fell in love with it and fed it anything
It would eat including raspberries made hard
By the lateness of the season
And dusty with the road.

It requires nice people to raise nice animals
And we were among them; a Bostonian
With a visceral hatred for the St. Louis
Cardinals, but otherwise fine. He had
Motor-homed half the universe
With his wife and why not?
She was an extremely nice woman.

Hot chocolate was to be had there for free
And tea and something called Instant
Coffee. The camps were nothing special
But they were cheap, the ocean showed
Between hills on the Digby Neck
And at night the whales crossed the harbour
And vented from their blowholes.

GET REAL

With everything that's happening
do you really think it's the right time
to have a meaningful conversation with your wife?

The coffee's gone cold. The dog is dead.
In fact there hasn't been a dog since
the Mahoney brothers were convicted

of that double homicide, and now you want to get
all touchy feely with your wife?
You're not even legally married.

THE LOST WALLETS OF THE ELDERLY

Exhaustion
Has entered my eyes
I am loveless
In my chair before the TV
The TV cares nothing for me.

But I was desired once
When desire swept the ranks
Of men and they arrived
In great ships like warriors
In legends.

I had passions
That darkened
With each trip
To the doctor's
Office.

The stars lost their shine
The revolution failed
Then suddenly the police phoned
And my wallet was not lost
Anymore.

THE THING THAT SHE WORE

Whenever she wore the thing he couldn't tolerate
he went into the hills and vented his madness.
A cross between a figure skater's leotard
and a Mexican sombrero the thing that she wore
was too much for him.

Even the gods pushed themselves away
from their screens and took notice. They were forever
descending from their heavenly condominiums
and demanding that she wear the thing
and then getting her pregnant.

Eventually she grew tired of wearing the thing.
"It doesn't fit anymore," she said. "I'm too fat,"
and she changed into more of a loose-fitting
floral thing which incited little or no madness
in the minds of men and allowed her to breathe
more easily.

Now it was the gods' turn to go into the mountains
and vent their madness. The man however found it safe to return
and lie with her on a king-sized mattress. He was no longer mad.
He was no longer anything; just another man
who occasionally entertained memories of how attractive
his wife had been when they were young.

WHAT'S HAPPENING

They came across the field by the lake
a woman and her two young daughters
neither of them women yet but both prepared
for what might happen next.

They skirted the warning track of a baseball game
in progress, walking slowly beneath the lighting stanchion
where the ospreys nested.

Between the chatter of baseball and the chitter
of small birds they came to watch the last inning
of the game. The umpire was late; there'd been
a tragic accident on the Lakeshore coming into the city
a bicyclist was killed and the section of highway
was cordoned off with yellow emergency tape.

Their father's team was winning for once.
He was old now and laughable in the field and they derided him
with affection. By the time the game was over the sun
had been slugged high into right field and hung there
on its way down behind the Princes' Gates.

Nothing was more beautiful they thought; the orange of it,
the flame and coloured candle wax of sunset,
the sepulchral statue of a brooding angel
that crouched over the Exhibition grounds.

And over them rose the towers where people
lived behind glass, high above the earth
where they never took a pitch for a called third strike
or had to shout at their deteriorating parents grown deaf
with age and fearful of what was happening to them.

RAINOUT AT CORONATION PARK

We huddled beneath makeshift shelters
in the rain taking selfies as the sky
tore itself into pieces and died coughing
on the green outfield of Coronation Park.

Oh Suzanna was knocked unconscious
here by a fly ball, Pete died, he tried
to kill me once with a baseball bat but
stopped himself. A woman was involved.
Pete died young.

A boy without a name
revealed his sexual orientation too early
and fled screaming from the intimacies
that follow games. Beers and fish tacos
hung on our breath but we cursed
and fought, and became pregnant

and gave birth to baseball and were
blessed with many eureka moments
but we died in service to the game
or from drinking or came back
from the edges of our graves

with a medallion that celebrated
sobriety, a woman and even
our children once again willing
to speak to us. We grew old on that green
spread of earth, occasionally
we turned two or fumbled fly balls
in spectacular fashion but mostly
our joints stiffened and our kids

went deep into video and
we did not know what to do;

two out, woman on third, bottom
of the fifth, down by six, the world
struggles with that situation
but not us. We sit
in makeshift shelters waiting
for the rain to end.

THE LINGUISTS

We have learned to interpret the *mew mews*
Of the cat as she patrols the vast estate
Of our matrimonial bed. "You have given me
The gift of family," says the cat "for which
I am grateful but now I'm hungry so feed me
And I don't mean that dry stuff either."

Even the washer and the dryer
Insist on their linguistic privileges;
They sing a song of voltages and currents, turning
Head over heels, underpants gone akimbo
In the electric orgy of machines.

THE LANGUAGE OF CROWS

I have come to understand
the language of crows. I'm not saying
that I comprehend every last caw
just that overall I get the gist
of it. Mostly it concerns sex
and food and matters like that
though occasionally it ventures
into what we might loosely
call the mythic or the symbolic
level of verbal expression. Those
fast, machine-like repetitions
fired off from the pinnacle
of a black spruce I believe
represent an incipit, like call me
Ishmael or the way Seamus
Heaney opens his translation of Beowulf
with the word "so." So, says the crow,
let this day begin, let the water
wash the shore,
let those things I eat
render themselves unto me. Otherwise
the rest of it is mimicry of the Latin Vulgate,
imitations of Dante and the early
Tuscan poets with some Germanic
gutturals thrown in for effect.

QUESTION MARKS

Have we become old then me to you
You to me? Have the great years crashed
In thunder and will memory
Gather in puddles on the church parking lot
In the morning with the moms
And the occasional dads who come
To deposit their kids in the daycare?
Is that it? The white shirt I wore
Rolled at the sleeves that left you
Defenseless banished from even
The Salvation Army basement bin?
Your legendary lime green underwear
Removed for the last time to lie
In that much-protested land-fill
Pressed beneath the microwave ovens
And the scorched mattresses?

WIFE

There's a woman sleeping beside me
I presume to be my wife, or someone
similar to a wife. There is certainly
something wife-like about the way she lies there.
She has been there for almost as long
as I can remember and shows no indication
of packing her bags anytime soon. I suspect
it's too late for dramatic exits. She says
her name is Deborah but whose wife she is
is not clear. It has entered my mind
more than once that she is *my* wife.
The phrase has a certain comfort to it;
"This is my wife" I might say to someone
who has experience with these things, and receive
understanding in return or maybe not.
What if she is only my wife by accident?
What if she is the wife of Bath or the wife
of someone with shadowy connections
to the underworld? What then?

YESTERDAY

Things are better today
than yesterday
thank god

Yesterday
with its circumstances
and failed romances
was enough to kill
an elephant

Maybe not the elephant
that's made itself at home
in my living room
but most elephants

Let's just say
yesterday is no longer
relevant

If I can live
with an elephant
in my living room
I can live

with what happened
yesterday.

THE HOUSE CLEANING

What we did to each other in these rooms
With the unforgiveable wallpaper
And the Mediterranean sunset paintings
Has passed into history:
Dad died his mysterious death
Down the hall; the uneaten food
In the cat bowls grows green and fuzzy.

Every door lock has been pried open
By a screwdriver inserted by a troubled
Young woman whose tragic past raced
Without hesitation into a tragic future.
If these rooms proved anything
It was that the future is always a memory
Of what went wrong.

So much went wrong even though the requisite
Number of babies were born here, novels written,
Wills executed, threats made. Wine was drunk, milk
Spilled, cheques kited, cats petted, wounds licked.
Love was made and so was an origami dinosaur
Assembled by a classical guitarist who played
Left-handed.

Then house prices went through the roof
And the bonds of matrimony
Were found to be in conflict with the zoning by-laws.
The furnace kicked out on the coldest day of winter
And everything else including the typewriter
With the keys that stuck incessantly

...

And the books that festered in boxes
In the basement, the thingamajigs
That once constituted the architecture
Of our love have now passed
Beyond recognition and can barely be
Given away for free at a yard sale.

THE FUTURE HAD NOTHING TO DO WITH IT

We spoke with some eloquence
Back then when the years
Hadn't broken apart
And the two of us began
Our journey to the north.

There were no children in those years
When we aimed binoculars at the shore
In search of a place to put in.
The children were not born yet so the coast
Was clear to travel old roads the future
Had nothing to do with.

Time was all we had to spend really
But we had enough of it to walk through
A constellation of fireflies.
There were so many fireflies

In those nights
When the rain nattered against the tin
And we were on the mattress
In each other's arms.

ICARUS

I've never fallen in love so much
As climbed into it head first
My arms hauling me up the horrible slope
My knees scraped to the bone
My bones broken, my heart a mess
My memoirs unpublished, my life
An unfathomable disaster, my cat
With fleas. You get the picture.

I've never fallen in love so much
As taken an elevator to the top floor
And knocked softly at the door
Wanting in, wanting love, wanting
A place to sleep, wanting something
To eat, wanting a bed on which to let my dreams
Out to pasture.

FREE RANGE HUSBANDS

ELECTION NIGHT AT THE RHINOCEROS TAVERN

In the Rhinoceros Tavern we drink
and call upon America to change.
We will not bless her bullets nor accept
cut rate postal service just because we're told
we need to stay young forever.
Hell no, we're here, we're drinking beer,
some of us are queer and some are neither this
nor that but we stand as one for what we believe in
which is flexible to say the least.

The candidate is thirty-two and wearing bondage heels.
She has toe cleavage and a post-doc from the London School
of Economics. The opposition didn't stand a chance.
No one in this joint is more than human, no one
is forced to kneel to the tyrannical dance move.
We eat and drink with impunity, the votes are in, the die
is cast. All we need now is for the world to stick out its thumb
and hitch a similar ride.

There are gentle women here of exceptional beauty
their very cheekbones uphold the principles by which we live.
There is not a glass of beer that does not portend a future filled
with free dental care and meaningful employment for the young.
Babies will be made tonight in the aftermath of our victory
but we will not justify our adulterous ways as a response
to dark times. The guacamole dip has never tasted better,
the fries are not bad. Last call is still several hours off.
Nothing can stop us after tonight.

FREE RANGE HUSBANDS

I married a free range husband after reading a book
titled *Men Who Run with the Aid of a Walking Stick*
"If you don't want to marry a dick, read this book."
That's what it said on the cover and being literary by nature
I bought the book and hated it. Who needs another
desperate self-help book published by some desperate
former school-teacher turned relationship guru
trying to make a buck from writing about what she learned
from her mistakes? Really.

Anyway, I married the guy and it wasn't exactly roses.
He'd written a slew of high-end literary novels that no one
liked except me, although I did get three kids out of him
the last one adopted, and he took me north of Chapleau
once where I saw the most stunning displays of northern lights
you could ever imagine and almost by accident caught
a twenty-six pound pike on *his* fishing rod when I was
really just trying to catch itty bitty sunfish with the kids.

The rest was mixed. He developed a drinking problem
that took him twenty years to kick and I opened
a small psychotherapy practice where I listened to people
talk about how depressed they were. The kids grew up
and refused to move out. "We love you guys too much"
they said, "forget about it." So now we're all jammed
into this little house, texting and sexting and doing laundry
five times a day and shouting at each other and playing
Snakes 'n' Ladders like we used to do when we were
foolish children.

COMMUNITY BARBARIANS

By the time I was old enough to be
young and beautiful it was too late;
the barbarians had pulled up to the gate
and were abusing my family.

They called my wife overweight
they said my children should be put back
in the orphanage where they came from.
"There are no orphanages," I said. "You mean
foster homes," but being barbarians
they had no interest in the
adoption system.

They were not the sort of people
who split hairs. Skulls maybe, they'd split
your skull, but they were not the sort
of people you want writing poetry
in front of your house.

BAD HAIR LIFE

Having cultivated a tragic hairdo
he had difficulty letting go of it

Everything was doom and destruction
and down payment on a house you could

count on being haunted. His forelock
would not shut up about incurable cancers

and getting stabbed in the back by best friends.
He was an anchor around his wife's neck

Why don't you get a haircut she said
but the demands of bad hair are merciless

and his tirades against proto-fascist organic food
and celebrity authors continued until finally

he went bald and his opinions
no longer fell from his head.

MISTRALS ONE AND TWO

I

"Scratch my back," she instructed
"there, no, lower, right, lower
you missed it. You have lost your chops,"
she said and went back to her electronic reader
and detective so-and-so with his analytical mind
and eccentric habits.

II

"Good god," said the woman whose life
had been ruined by her husband. "You'd think in this
day and age they could prevent macular degeneration
by putting something over the screen."
"They can. But they *won't*," said the other woman
whose life had not been ruined by her husband
but had not been much improved by it either.

MR. RELIABLE

My wife has claimed me for herself
the foolish woman. Even my children
are expressing an uncomfortable degree
of attachment as if they're counting on me
to be there when it matters.

And when it matters they'll find me
on the bed giving my full attention
to the ceiling. I'm not a heartless man

I've given to the poor and even
if my attempts to steal from the rich
never landed me the book deal
that writers kill for

I still give a quarter to the odd
sidewalk junkie whose claim
to have fallen on hard times falls
mostly on deaf ears.

This doesn't make me a saint
it just means that families are not
for the faint-hearted; as soon
as you put the cat down the kids
scream bloody murder.

THE FALL OF ROME

Just when the canapés have been set down on the table
we discover that Rome has been sacked
and that Jane and Richard's separation has grown
increasingly acrimonious. The wine, the good stuff
is in the kitchen with the hostess. "What wonderful
black fish-net stockings you're wearing," I say,
"are they your daughter's?" "No," she laughs,
"they're mine." We kiss like Europeans, once
on each side of the face. It's taken me ten years
to learn this little trick.

Her husband is raving mad, he believes the entire world
can be comprehended in the contours of a bread tab
And her, don't be fooled by that double French kiss
and the fish-nets. She once hauled beer in a North Bay
tavern frequented by bikers and knows how to put a tattoo
on a sailor's belly with a straight razor. Face it, these women
know their way around. We were undergraduates
at a small midwestern college when they were getting groped
by television personalities and setting the world on fire.

Having written his doctoral thesis on Milton's *Aeropagitica*,
the professor installed a young man in his house
to set down the canapés on the table. There's nothing
like a little bit of shortbread to bring out the Scottish in people.
I watched him pour himself an eye-popping glass
of Scotch. I'm not talking a double here, I mean a double
squared to the umpteenth degree, my goodness

that man can drink. Seventy-nine years old and always eager
to talk dirty, or just talk. "And you?
Are you not suspiciously beautiful for a woman of your age?
Please allow me to introduce myself," I said, "I'm a man of –"
"Of course you are," she interrupted and went off
to another corner of the room where they were
discussing Dewey-style pragmatism.

CONUNDRUM

My husband thinks that I'm a genius and why not?
When I was young he thought I was hot and now
that I'm not young he's sneaking around with that
dark-haired post-doc with the cheekbones up to here.

It turns out that he's only human too. What's a woman
to do under the circumstances except dress quickly
and get out while she can. Jimmy may crack corn
but he's been known to crack a few other things as well.

WITH OUR MOUTHS WIDE SHUT

Overnight the snow assembled
With dignity.
"How long have you been up?" she said
And he answered evasively. Life had gotten
Away from him and he felt rather foolish
About it. For her part she had squandered
A full decade and was certain it had come back
To haunt her. Although as far as he could tell
She was ghost-free.

It was the transitions between the exalted
And the tawdry that caught
In his throat; the things people felt justified
To say. Hardly anyone could afford
To keep their mouths shut anymore
Least of all his own which had been frequently
Shot off and left for dead.

COLD SNAP

This winter was more capable
Of killing than previous ones
All compassion fled from the instruments
That measure cold.

Our teeth chattered, our children
Left us, our parents withered beneath
Drifts of time in seniors' homes
that none of us could afford.

Even before the snow stopped
We were old and hoped for nothing better
Than a fried egg sandwich
With a cup of tea.

THE TOUCHERS

We touch too much. We do.
You touch me I touch you.
We touch and touch and touch
We touch tenderly we touch
Inappropriately. We touch too much

We do. Someone in a public position
Touches a person privately
And pays the price. We touch
Children on the hair. Animals too.
We touch too much. We do.

THE CREATIVES

He went from being heteronormative
to phallogocentric in the time it took
to make a ham and cheese sandwich
for the homeless. "I didn't even know
the homeless were *allowed* to eat meat,"
said the video artist driving daddy's
new car. He had recently fallen
in love with her. Married
with children, plush of figure, over
thirty-five with a vocal fry and a place
in the country, she was everything
he dreamed of in a woman.

He was a dreamer and always had been.
She was a scenester who had recently
become a hipster and could handle a tube
of lipstick like an assassin. Twenty years
of professional heart-breaking she knew
how to handle a het like him. It ended
badly the way these millennial mix-ups do.
She was rushed to the emergency ward
as she had been so many times before.
He continued working with the homeless
and drifted deeper into problems of his own.

THE CONCOCTION

I thought I would concoct
A story so familiar that whoever
Told the story or wrote it down
Or pretended to find it in a bottle floating
In Lake Michigan wouldn't matter.

A story that turned out to be the mother
Of stories which, if we're being honest,
Is always a story about someone's mother.
Your mother or the mother
Of a brilliant Venetian poet who wrote
His greatest work in a language that he
Invented himself. How do we know it's
So bloody brilliant then, you ask?
Which is a good question.

In fact it all turned out to be a fraud.
The Venetian poet was not a Venetian
He was from Calgary and he
Was in the oil business and never wrote
A poem in his life. He did a few crossword
Puzzles and wondered if there wasn't
Some big mystery that lay at the heart
Of everything but beyond that
We know very little about the man.

DRIVING WITH CAB

I found myself in a cab
With Cab Calloway of all people
Driving along the boulevard of jazz
Of all places, tapping what I thought
Was a decent beat on the bottom
Of the steering wheel when
The great man said
"Stop here kid I gotta see a joker
About some business" and got out
And entered the side door of one of those
Establishments where the neon
Is always reflected upside down in a puddle.
The meter was running, he came out
Twenty minutes later in the company
Of a dark-haired woman who seemed to know
The ropes and flashed her teeth in the rear
View mirror as we drove away.

SWIMMING UNDER SOCIALISM

Who expected so much beauty
to be floating around in a public pool
with four lifeguards and even a leg
to stand on? Half naked, three quarters
undressed, largely unaffected,
up to the neck in this, heart-broken
by that, everybody's asses hanging out,
moms and dads getting away
from their god-awful kids
for an afternoon, this is what it means
to live large poolside in the big time;
all the micro-bikini girls are *summa cum*
laude and the guys haven't cracked
a book since *The Hounds of the Baskervilles*
but so what? It's a heat wave and even
the old man with the caved-in chest
is doing a cannonball.

WHAT PRICE LIFE

As the crow flies so do we
not into the sky so much as into
some raucous place where the men get louder
with each drink and the women insist
on dancing to Van Morrison.

It turns out our skin is not as thick
as we thought it was; no sooner has someone mocked us
on social media than our heads are in the oven
along with the frozen lasagna.

Death stares us in the face but that
is the least of our worries.
Common sense has made a mess
of things. They say even the Internet
is not reliable.

UNDER THE CIRCUMSTANCES

Things have not been going very well for me lately.
My friends have noticed something defective
In my personality, my loved ones have succumbed
To the usual diseases and are either bed-ridden or too burdened
By our approaching doom to even sit down for coffee.

Nonetheless the cat sneaks out the door the moment I open it.
The birds remain insistent that we delay our suicide
For one more day. The sun is still forceful.
The tap leaks, and a gang of teenage thugs sneaks
From one house to another in the hope of stealing something
That can be exchanged for dope. In other words
Things are not as bad as even good people say they are.

TO HELL WITH MR. BARTUZZI

What a predicament to find yourself in;
Stricken by grief from the neck down;
Your house in hock; both your major
And minor works out of print; your one
Good pair of blue jeans no longer fitting
Because your ass has gone flat.

Who then should step out of the elevator
But Mr. Bartuzzi; walking, talking proof
of why we should sit still and keep quiet.
He wants to know if the eggs Benedict
Were to your satisfaction.

So you explain to him curtly
That satisfaction is not on your agenda
The eggs had blood in the yokes
And you are attempting to deal
With a crippling addiction that killed your mother
And shows every sign of destroying you as well.

Ah yes, he says and spritzes his face
With a small bottle of lavender water.
In that moment you realize
There's already enough hate in the world
And that you will not let a lousy plate
Of eggs Benedict and that god awful
Lavender smell ruin your day.

MONOGAMISTS IN LOVE

She bought me so many coffees
That by the time she was done with me
We had exhausted both radical feminism
And how having large breasts at the age
Of fifteen had affected her development
As a woman.

Meanwhile, people were shouting
Their heads off in all directions
About all things but mostly
About matters of equity and not
Being loved enough.

Show me someone who's been loved enough
And I will show you someone
Who spent half his life head first
In a bottle and then against all odds

Spent the other half coaching
His daughter's baseball team
To a provincial championship.

Which is not to say the woman
Has no regrets. Thirty years with a
Dipstick like him, she learned a little
Something about men.

START WITH A WOMAN

Start with a woman, why not?
Who doesn't?
Start with a woman
And you're half-way to being alive.
If you are nice to a woman
She will give birth to you
If you are not nice to a woman
She may still give birth to you
But you will be a monster
Maybe not a monster
But you will never cuddle
Against a woman in a bed
Made of solemn promises
And laughter. You'll never sleep
On a mattress made of flesh and affection
Or have your fears allayed
By her presence in a bed
Made of compassion.
Try sleeping in a bed
without compassion, mister.
See where that gets you.
Start with a woman, why not?
Who doesn't?

READING LIFE

HOW TO START A POEM

You can start anywhere really
That awkward awards ceremony for example
Where all those white-skinned authors
Assured us the book was not dead
"Yeah? Well what about you?" shouted
Some drunken wit from the peanut gallery
And there was to say the least
An uncomfortable silence until the host
A radio announcer by trade who lived in fear
Of dead air, spewed forth such a tirade
Of platitudes that she was immediately
Honoured with the Order of the British Empire
But my god the food was good; everything
Was *au gratin* and everybody was going *ooh la la*
And indicating to the waiters that they wanted
More wine.

THE COUNTRY WELL

When I was a boy I fell into a well
A country well boarded over so that boys
Like me could crash through and come face
To face with spiders and the muck that lies
Inside of things or just beneath them.

From that black hole
I was laughed at – by God I thought – who made
Muck and spiders and little boys
Get their come-uppance when they least expected it.

Part of me remains in that hole
With the muck and spiders
But part of me got out to fall again,
This time in love with a woman
Who had no tolerance for men who fell
Into dark places that they were eager
To fathom and probably write books about.

"Either you get yourself out of the muck
Or you find someone else to go to bed with,"
She said, so I climbed out of the well into which
I had fallen and fell in love with her instead.

Now we have a house with kids and cats
And if I write books at all I limit myself
To bestsellers and save my real work
For the muck and spiders and God's
Disapproving eyeball that stares down
On that stuck little boy.

THE FATAL SKIN

I tried it once, I did, I threw the kids
Into the trunk of the car and did
What mothers do in the news.
Straight into the lake I went
With the kids in the trunk
And a copy of Balzac's
The Fatal Skin on the car seat
Beside me. In retrospect
I should have done it the other way
Around, the kids beside me
And Balzac in the trunk
But there is something about
A water-damaged book
That depresses me beyond belief.
In the end it didn't matter because
At the last minute I swerved
From the precipitous precipice
And went to the Dairy Queen instead
Where the kids had a pralines and cream
Milkshake and I sat on a picnic table
Reading Balzac, and experiencing
What he calls an almost feminine yearning
For Oriental languor.

HELLS BELLS

Who says of hell that nobody
goes there anymore? Sure, the place
is packed, the service is slow
and sometimes disrespectful

but those who bad-mouth hell
in fact have never been to hell;
maybe they attended some disagreeable
family function that went on too long

but they spent no hellish hours
imprisoned in their soul
reading books that make you feel
dirty the moment you put them down.

THE INFINITE PARK

It was the hottest day of the year
and those arrived from war-torn places
played in the park with coloured balls and barbecues.
A man strummed guitar by himself on a bench.
He didn't care if anyone listened. The notes
leapt into the steaming air like bird seed
chucked to a starving flock and somewhere
Shakespeare was enunciated from an outdoor stage.

Terrible things had happened. Words were spoken
that could not be taken back. Long walks
were had that went nowhere and resolved nothing.
The heat made it clear that even nature hated us.
It was the hottest day of the year
and everything had fallen apart.

There were homeless people in the park
and people who were not homeless but powerless
just the same. Two women played tennis
in the encroaching dark. Joggers jogged
but ended up no further from themselves
than when they started. Each of our solitudes
had come to the park to cool off on the hottest
day of the year knowing the limitations of the park
were infinite but still willing to risk it.

JUSTICE REPORT WITH LOVE APPENDED

If you're waiting for justice
To run a victory lap
Around this joint maybe
You should take another pill
Maybe you should consider
Ordering another bottle of champagne
Even though you have no way
Of paying for the first one.
Only criminals
Get to milk the cows on this farm
Criminals and high-flying
Elaborately interesting people for whom
Everything is effortless, may God
Prick their skin with tasers
And may the missing girls and women
Of the highways emerge safe
From the back seats
Of cop cars.
Justice makes it abundantly clear
Where gratitude comes from;
From the belly when there's food
In it. From park swings at night
When kids launch themselves
Into the harvest moon.

READING LIFE

The son falls asleep on the sofa following
a heavy afternoon meal with beer and the mom
makes exquisite small talk across the generations.
This is what you would expect from a life that is largely
based on books. The son, of course will be revealed
to be indolent and selfish, mom will have no end
of addictions. Disappointed in love she has turned
her unfulfilled needs on her son etc. who in turn
etc. etc. But wait, there's more. A chance at love?
You bet. Here comes that finely wrought flashback
in which love was there for the taking but was not
taken. The moral being that you should never
(surprise surprise) turn your back on love.

WHITE MALE BRITISH AUTHORS FROM THE SIXTIES

What boozers they were, those
Bird-chasing British authors made
Of white skin and marmalade. How
Heavily they hit the sauce and how haughtily
They scorned Americans, Armenians,
Spaniards and anyone with a mid-European
Accent. Great seducers of faculty wives
Their cheerful hatred of women had a breezy
Boys' club quality that set the tone
For what came later. Dreadful parents,
Worse husbands, drooled over
In the pages of the *Times Literary Supplement*,
Finally their choleric, scotch-spotted
Faces stopped showing on the backs of books
And the world was free of them.

THE COMPETITION

The poet's name was Ian
and he is dead now in the way
that poets are, but he was articulate
about subway graffiti,
soulless landlords, and the fallen leaves
where city poets find their truth.

I felt in his work the pain
of poets etc., at least the dark
arrogance that comes from being
both dead broke and brilliant
at the same time. He had nothing
to eat but who did back then?
When the lies of our fathers hung
like the lowest lying fruit

and we were too busy plucking them
to hold down a job. What empire
did not have the rug pulled out
from under it by the likes of us?
What undergraduate beauty
could ever sleep without first nurturing
the troubled genius that was in us?
Quite a few of them, it turned out.
Even Melanie who married
a mailman when she was twenty-two.

ELIZABETH SMART

Having packed a few sandwiches and changed
the batteries on the old woman's medical alert machine
that hung around her neck, she sat down by Grand Central
Station and wept. And why not? Four kids for God's sake
wandering about war-torn Europe mooning for the guy
and pregnant to boot. "You ever meet a man like that
you don't sit down by Grand Central Station and weep.
You rip his balls off, do you hear me?"

This is the sort of advice that a mother gives
to her fifteen-year-old daughter. Sure, there had been
affairs, his mostly, some peculiar activities took place
behind the furnace in the basement of a restaurant.
But the rest of it was the regular church and empire stuff.
Once or twice she sat down under his shadow
with great delight but for the most part there was no reason

to keep getting pregnant. And you would have thought
she knew better than to get lippy with an Arizona cop
with a copy of the Mann Act stuffed down his pants.
But no matter how well-heeled she was, no matter how white
and well-connected, it still had to hurt when her father
used his diplomatic connections to get her lover stopped
at the border, and her mother campaigned successfully
to have her book banned in Canada.

PANCAKE BAY

We flung ourselves into one textual moment after another
and all we got for it was the privilege of fetching the Big Guy
a glass of wine at one of those book events that big guys
feel obliged to attend. The giants of literature were
there again, feeling extremely good about themselves
and putting their hands on the backsides of young women
while their wives and daughters stared stonily across the room.
What brilliance was there and sensitivity, so much sensitivity
that we fled down the fire escape in the hope of staying young
    forever.
Instead the other thing happened.

You know what comes next. We will end up at a baseball
tournament in Illinois cheering on this or that child
when the sky opens and all the lap dancers
who live in heaven give us the finger for our lifetime
of meagre gratuities and we go home with a trophy
and a renewed respect for American hospitality but
we will have aged and nothing will taste like it did
when we cooked whitefish on the beach at Pancake Bay.

POETRY TOWN

Our town is not the sort of place
Where poetry can just walk down the street
And not get accosted by the brothers Mahoney.
Even if one of the brothers is known
To have a gun we understand that poetry
Doesn't lend itself to the sort of violence
We've come to expect: poetic violence for sure,
Abusive poetry, poetry that gets drunk
And says things that are difficult to forget.
But poetry armed with a gun is not
Acceptable in our town.

In our town there's no difference
Between a soft machine and a soft parade.
Yes, the police are dreadful editors;
Dull, uneducated men with guns
And hulking fists who don't know
A sestina from a triolet.
We understand they have a job to do.

Probably the brothers Mahoney
Are running another high stakes
Poker game in a rented house
With a blanket stretched across the window
But in the basement it's all Ferlinghetti
And Elizabeth Bishop smoking like mad
And hanging out in our town;

Halfway between the hip hop and the doo wop
Between Miles Davis and Mrs. Slopecki
Who appears in her front door at midnight
Handing out homemade cookies
To anyone who will have them.

THE LESSON OF THE MASTER

Because she was first and foremost a poet, children
were not an option. She would pursue diphthongs
over diapers; the babbling brooks of poetic discourse
took precedence over the bawling idiocy of babies
which is fine. Her verses were polished in solitude;
acclaim followed as did a series of literary awards
that she mounted on her mantle like the portraits
of beloved family members. The years passed,
her poetry became increasingly tight, insightful
and ultimately she managed a part-time engagement
as a creative writing instructor at a prestigious
Canadian university. She had no hell-bent
and hysterical teenage daughter to scream at her
or to run away from home for three days and nights
so the police had to be called and a loud
and melodramatic reconciliation take place
on the front lawn. She instead had the collected works
of Anne Sexton (one of them signed)
and a picture of herself standing next to Neruda
when it was still acceptable to do that.
Then she hit something of a dry spell
and purchased two pet turtles to help her
with the sometimes crushing loneliness
that comes to those who dedicate themselves
to the intricacies of art. One of them
contracted mange and died almost immediately
but the other crawled about for decades
in a fern-filled aquarium and provided no end
of inspiration for her. Her turtle poetry
was considered among the best ever written
about turtles in any language. When it came
to the miniature pet turtle in particular

she was said to be without peer. Now she lives
in an assisted-care facility near Whitby,
Ontario and once a day she gets outside
with the help of an aluminum walker.

WHAT IS POETRY WITHOUT LOVE

Of course he was faithful to the Muse
Of course he was not faithful to the women

Only after the Muse had been taken care of
would he even consider getting down the Easy Off

and giving the oven a good clean. He liked
a little obscene banter with the women

of course he did. Back then none of it stayed forever
on a hard drive put there by Russian agents

It just came and went. Like him
scot-free. He was a Scotsman. Nothing

wrong with that, no reason to make a haggis joke
He was a protegé of T.S. Eliot's. No reason

to hold that against him either, but the thing
about the women, the women and, the "Jews,"

"blistered in Brussels" and all that "spawning," stuff
it was not good, it never is. He was faithful to his Muse however

and sometimes his Muse demanded
that he mentor a young student in the art of love.

ENOUGH WITH SHELLEY ALREADY

(from "Prometheus Unbound")

What a prodigious guy really, so melancholy
forever surrounded by armorial beasts
and sepulchered emblems and things like that.

Between the vaporous exultations
and the cloven fire crags, it makes you wonder
when he had any time to write poetry.

And all that free love? It must have cost the guy
a fortune. All it takes is one boney chain jammed
in the hard black deep and the next thing you know

there you are on the slimy shore getting gobbled
by summer worms on a maggoty corpse while this guy
is carrying on like some crystal paramour for God's sake.

SOME PEOPLE ARE CAPABLE OF BEING REALISTIC BUT YOU'RE NOT ONE OF THEM

Despite being a realist I have worn my underwear
backwards more than once. I have assembled peanut butter
and jam sandwiches during the witching hour and consumed them
under the influence Thomas à Kempis's *The Imitation of Christ*,

When my head was turned by a head considerably prettier
than mine I went nuts and stayed that way for six years.
Realism had nothing to do with it or maybe it did. Maybe
I was just being realistic when I collected her pink ribbons

and hanged myself with them. Dead or alive I attempted
to have my head screwed on straight. I was certainly not
one of those men who acted foolishly in the presence
of female beauty. Ask my wife if you don't believe me

my ex-wife, I mean. My reach always extended beyond
my grasp. Having been taught from an early age that this
is what heaven was for I lost the tip of my baby finger
in a door my sister shut on it. Shut doors mean nothing

if you're a realist. I simply knock them against my forehead
until they finally agree with me. And if they don't
I make a point of not staying where I'm not wanted at least
not until the police are called and I'm dragged out of there.

THE POETRY OF FREDERICK SEIDEL

for Frederick Seidel

I've never been anywhere really
certainly not to the Via della Spiga
not to Milan. I went to San Francisco once
and got a parking ticket. I went up the street
to my buddy Jack's and smoked dope.

But that certainly wasn't me you saw whipping
down the Via Borgospesso on a Ducati.
As to that whole "ravishing women" thing, sure
there was a time, I guess. My wife was once considered
to have the nicest bum in the city. I'm not sure

who gets to determine that? How do you get to be
on that jury? All those young poets, I guess,
with their scarves and upturned collars attempting
to sweep her off the dance floor. They've all gone
into limbo now. Or advertising.

WHO WAS THAT GUY?

That elegant European met at a dinner party who had passed the prime of his life and was free now to appreciate a woman with a well-intentioned but slightly awkward gesture, nothing so gauche as kissing the back of her hand of course but an audible sigh as one might utter after witnessing an extraordinary sunset, a man possessed of a certain dignity that comes of being loved three times, each time by a goddess, and by reading again the great books of his life, and who informs you that years ago he climbed the five floors of a New York brownstone to introduce himself to Djuna Barnes simply to inhale, as he put it, the dust of her bitterness. Even the weave of his clothing suggested he was on a first name basis with maître d's of storied restaurants. An air of dignified failure surrounded him, an aura of compelling distraction as he remembered years ago when he entered the bedroom of the two Canadian girls who were still warm and lazy from their love-making, the one who smiled at him and covered herself with one hand and with the other offered up a small dish of hallucinogenic mushrooms served in yogurt. Welcome to Canada she said.

READING HABITS OF THE DEAD

Lying in bed with a book
Above my face I fret no more
Over the disappearance
Of everything that made nostalgia
Worth living for.

Cancer, of course, and cops
Who kill occupy
The low-rent regions of my mind.
Starvation and a life on the streets
Remain a distinct possibility.

But lying in bed with a book
It's clear to me that only the dead
Have things to worry about.
My overdue library book might gnaw
At my conscience but the dead

Have no borrowing privileges whatsoever
And are forced to read those unrelenting
Blockbuster family saga novels
That people leave behind at the cottage.

HEART FELT

There's a story written on my heart
where I can't read it. Imagine that
me, who read everything in sight
can't read a damn thing when it's written
on my heart.

The language of the story
is not easy to understand.
It relies heavily on the genitive case.
Every verb has nine major conjugations.
There is no punctuation. There is no telling
if the story is a true story
or just something that appeared
because it was a slow news day.

Of course my heart on which this story
Is written is broken. Whether it is broken
in two, or three, or six or God knows
how many pieces, I'm not sure.

But it might explain
Why it is so difficult for me to read the story
That is written on my heart.

A HISTORY OF

Being barely a few words in the index
Of a book that was never written is enough
To make you wonder what all the fuss was about.
All that twisting and shouting in the rec rooms
Of a squeaky clean generation may have landed us
A nuclear family but it didn't stop the bomb
From going off.

Luckily love was not absent
Even though I had trouble accommodating
Its presence. It set up house in a house
In which I had been homeless for some time
And gave me someone to cook for, someone
To have and to hold and to grow old with
Even though growing old is something
You do in solitude and when you try to talk about it
It's hard to find the words.

EVERY DAY ENDS IN BED

Every day ends in bed, a book,
A cat, you making final taps at the keyboard
Kids fast asleep, cars below the window
Throwing off the watery noise of cars on pavement.

We are ready now, you and I,
After a day of making sandwiches and global
Conflict, to draw the curtain
On the helter and the skelter. Night
Has come like a pipe full of opium.

We are made stupid by it but not unconscious.
Soon there will be visits to the radiologist
And other appointments that must be kept.
The flesh will be more ravaged than it was
Twenty minutes ago, time will be more treacherous

But you will be next to me then
With a novel about police procedures
And I will slip from the nervous day
Into the warm shadows of your body.

The night will end like the rest of them
In light, in birdsong, in the ringing sound
Of children dropped off early to the Montessori
School across the street.

ACKNOWLEDGEMENTS

My deepest thanks to all the staff at Cormorant Books. My thanks also to Robyn Sarah, and to the editors and staff at *Queen's Quarterly*, for their interest and support.

PHOTO DEBORAH CLIPPERTON

Peter Unwin is the author of nine previous books, as well as many short stories, essays, and poems. His 2014 story collection *Life Without Death* was shortlisted for the 2014 Trillium Book Award, and his poetry collection *When We Were Old* was a Relit Award finalist. Peter is a member of PEN Canada.

The author can be reached at unwin@sympatico.ca .

POETRY FROM CORMORANT BOOKS

Undercurrents: New Voices in Canadian Poetry (Robyn Sarah, editor, 2011)

No End in Strangeness: New and Selected Poems (Bruce Taylor, 2011)

Some Frames (Jack Hannan, 2011)

The Other Side of Ourselves (Rob Taylor, 2011)

The Jonas Variations: A Literary Séance (George Jonas, 2011)

Ash Steps (M. Travis Lane, 2012)

Waking in the Tree House (Michael Lithgow, 2012)

Tilt (E. Blagrave, 2012)

The Port Inventory (Donald McGrath, 2012)

All the Daylight Hours (Amanda Jernigan, 2013)

A Bee Garden (Marilyn Gear Pilling, 2013)

A Rhythm to Stand Beside (Jack Hannan, 2013)

Hungry (Daniel Karasik, 2013)

Looking East Over My Shoulder (Jill Jorgenson, 2014)

When We Were Old (Peter Unwin, 2014)

Light Takes (Mia Anderson, 2014)

Crossover (M. Travis Lane, 2015)

Catullus's Soldiers (Daniel Goodwin, 2015)

Borrowed Days: Poems New and Selected (Marc Plourde, 2016)

Building on River (Jean Van Loon, 2018)

Giacometti's Girl (Sandra Davies, 2018)

Gods of East Wawanosh (Marilyn Gear Pilling, 2019)

We Were Like Everyone Else (Ken Victor, 2019)

Who We Thought We Were As We Fell (Michael Lithgow, 2021)

We acknowledge the sacred land on which Cormorant Books operates. It has been a site of human activity for 15,000 years. This land is the territory of the Huron-Wendat and Petun First Nations, the Seneca, and most recently, the Mississaugas of the Credit River. The territory was the subject of the Dish With One Spoon Wampum Belt Covenant, an agreement between the Iroquois Confederacy and Confederacy of the Anishinaabe and allied nations to peaceably share and steward the resources around the Great Lakes. Today, the meeting place of Toronto is still home to many Indigenous people from across Turtle Island. We are grateful to have the opportunity to work in the community, on this territory.

We are also mindful of broken covenants and the need to strive to make right with all our relations.